For Love of Life
and the Family

For Love of Life
and the Family

By Richard P. Delaney, M.D.

Serif Press
Pittsburgh
2020

Contents

Prologue..1

Introduction..3

Letter No. 1..5
  A Letter to My Own—The Problem of a
  World Seemingly Gone Mad Because Its
  Spiritual Well Has Gone Dry

Letter No. 2...37
  Answers to the Basic Questions of Life

Letter No. 3...65
  An Overview of How and Why the Family
  Has Been the Target of Evil Influence

Letter No. 4..74

The Amazing Biology Showing We Are
Wondrously Made: The Gift of Life—a
Life That Is Human

Tribute to Dr. Richard Delaney in the
Catholic Standard: "Dr. Richard Delaney
remembered for his love for his patients,
his faith"..82

Prologue

IN these pages you will meet a wonderful man—in fact, a great man—Dr. Richard P. Delaney. Dr. Delaney was a wonder in many ways. For one thing, he was a family physician who maintained a busy family practice for 60 years and often still made house calls—something almost unheard of today.

Early in his practice, he was instrumental in bringing hospice to the Washington, DC, area, traveling the Washington Beltway after office hours to the homes of terminally ill patients. He later introduced the hospice program to his local hospital, Holy Cross Hospital in Silver Spring, Maryland.

A modest man, gifted by his Creator with a brilliant intellect, he was chosen by his fellow physicians in the Washington area to author an open letter to the U. S. Supreme Court following the 1973 *Roe v. Wade* decision that imposed legalized abortion on the nation. His letter, published as a full-page newspaper ad, was paid for by his colleagues on the condition that he write it.

There is much else that could be said about Dr. Delaney, but it is best to let his own eloquent prose speak for itself. The pages that follow are excerpted from a series of letters he wrote to his first born great-granddaughter. Richard Delaney departed this earthly life October 28, 2018. A tribute that appeared in the *Catholic Standard* newspaper of November 29, 2018, is reprinted as a fitting close to this book.

> *R. Martin Palmer*
> *National Association for the*
>   *Advancement of Preborn Children*
> *21 Summit Ave,*
> *Hagerstown, MD 21740*
> *January, 2019*

Introduction

OUR world is severely challenged by a dominant religion—secularism. It has its clergy and its literature; you need only turn on your television set and—voilà! It has its prayer life; witness the countless hours spent at trivial yet frequently brutal mind-absorbing games. It has its televangelists; marketers spending countless billions in advertising endeavors scientifically geared to entrap your attention and encourage habits that will lead you to think their way.

Your own faith has become countercultural. It is now offensive to speak of God, death, sin, Heaven or Hell. Political correctness and not love of God is the order of the day. That is the catechism of secularism.

Richard P. Delaney, M.D.

Silver Spring, Maryland

December 2017

Letter No. 1

A Letter to My Own—
The Problem of a World Seemingly
Gone Mad Because Its Spiritual Well
Has Gone Dry

PERHAPS it is true: you never miss the water until the well runs dry. We need not be thirsty to realize the importance of water in our lives. We are made up mostly of water. It is vital to our personal as well as our communal existence. Wars have been fought and migrations of peoples motivated by our need for water. Yet whoever thinks of its grand status until its source is removed?

This is also true of air, warmth and many common needs only brought to mind by their absence. It is also true of the necessities of our moral makeup. Our very existence depends on a Creator who knows us and has mandated that we observe the laws He has built into our very nature. Yet He gives us freedom of will and thus the ability to decide to observe or to reject His natural law. Great and Noble religions have arisen from man's need to comply with his design.

God gave us the ability to reason not only that He exists, but also that He is infinitely perfect and powerful. At long last, He explicitly revealed himself and clearly mapped out the path we are to follow to achieve the goal, the life for which we were made.

Freedom of choice clearly implies the freedom to reject as well as to accept. Fallen angels who have decided to reject God have permanently rejected the will of our Creator. These enemies of God are alive and are operative in our world—in your world. They act out their hatred for the God Who Made Us by dimming His image and enticing us to concentrate on the "here" and the "now" and to ignore the "there" and "forever." The enemy is clever and tries, in a manner of speaking, to replace our life's water with his venom and to focus our attention on our thirst and our wants. Our final end—participation in the life of our Creator—and the means to achieve it are increasingly obscured.

As a society, we appear to have lost our grip on the belief in the existence of an almighty and transcendent God. God, who exists as a loving Community, Father, Son and Holy Spirit, created man in "His own image," which is to say: as meant to live within a loving familial Community. The family is the basic unit of our culture. Jesus' first two words in instructing His disciples on prayer in that instruction reflect this: "Our" (not "my")—referring to community—and "Father"—referring to the concept of family.

It doesn't require much in the way of social awareness to see that there is less and less room for God in the lives of our families. This social expulsion of the Almighty has been primarily manifested in the dissolution of the family itself.

It is within the family that belief in God is primarily engendered and nurtured, where virtue and the appetite for the good, the true and the beautiful are encouraged and strengthened. The family is the generator and primary teacher of the upcoming generation. Society looks to the family as its beacon of culture and morality.

The assault on the family is openly manifested and can be seen in many ways; not the least of which is the adverse effect exerted by our system of education upon our children's minds. It can be seen in our choices of leisure – i.e. a computer or television screen entrapping our attention for too many hours in empty but alluring ways. The family is also seriously threatened by the surrender of our basic freedoms to our government. Shortly, I will mention some of the more obvious cultural scars produced by the agents of change that deform us. The primary mechanisms by which by which external forces are injuring this sacred vital institution, the family, are, I believe, three: divorce, contraception and abortion.

Belief in the Transcendent has been under assault for two millennia. This assault has increased over the past two to three centuries as science has advanced dramatically while the teachings of our greatest philosophers and theologians have been and are being challenged.

The years from the birth of our country until now have witnessed major advances in scientific knowledge, massive industrialization, population growth and urbanization throughout the world. Secularism, relativism and tolerance-considered as virtues have become the order of the day. There has been a simultaneous loss of our Judeo-Christian heritage influencing education, religion and daily life. It must be said: The secularization of America is on the rise. The American family is on the ropes. Prompted by the birth of

our first great-granddaughter, Delaney Hart,
I address what I have to say as a letter to my
great-grandchildren and all related to them
by kith or kin. This is not meant to be a
philosophical, historical or scientific com-
mentary for I have no authority in any of
these fields. Least of all, is it to be seen as a
nostalgic look to the past, the "good old
days," seemingly happier and less burdened.
These were simply milestones on the devolu-
tionary downstream drift of our culture.

We appear to be moving relentlessly away
from our reassuring religious roots into a
world that now appears to grow more speed-
ily chaotic, crude and dangerous both
morally and physically.

The demise of the culture, however, need
not equate to the demise of the person.
Throughout history, there have always been
courageous, steadfast souls keeping the spirit
of truth alive in a world seemingly bent on its
own destruction. Consider first the early
martyrs and doctors of the Church. There has

also been a continuous emergence of heroes and heroines of the Word throughout the centuries. In our own day, I point to the likes of Mother Teresa and all of the popes in my lifetime who have expressed timeless truth to an unheeding world.

Seeing a vineyard after it has been harvested, cropped and pruned, one might imagine it has been destroyed. But roots and vines remain—unseen but ready to bring forth a new and abundant crop. The roots of our Faith carry the life of our moral inheritance, making it permanently accessible to all who determine to remain attached. It is my prayer now and forever—yes, "that vast forever"—that we will do that; that you will cling to the Everlasting Vine and thus remain ever and always a loving family. And so....

Dearest Darling Delaney Hart,

At the beginning of this writing, you were the youngest of my offspring and your big brother A.J. the only other of your generation. Another though, Aunt Sara's firstborn, is already on the way. Thus, my little one, while you were its inspiration, this letter is to you and to your cousins, parents, uncles, aunts and in fact all who owe their being to a very special wedding in St. Louis in 1954. It is also to any and all who might show interest in the ramblings and reminiscences of your great-grandfather Delaney.

My Generation has witnessed ever accelerating changes in our world, and the river of change appears to be increasing in volume and velocity. It is important to me then to point out to you what is and what was. What will be is up to you.

My hope is that I may help you to determine what you must preserve, what you must avoid and most importantly, the seed that you must plant to nourish Delaneys yet to come. And so I return to my happy memory, that very special wedding day 58 years ago.

It was three days after Christmas, December 28th, the Feast of the Holy Innocents.

That may seem remote to you, little one, but it is ever present to me and to my beautiful bride, your great-grandmother Joyce.

I was a sophomore in medical school and Christmas break was the only available time to get away for a few days. Neither of us had even the slightest doubt about what we were about to do. Our parents were much more circumspect (a colossal understatement).Joyce had graduated from College Misericordia in June with a degree in teaching. The thought of putting our wedding off until after my graduation we rejected outright. The wait would be too long and so we wed.

It was a small wedding as most of the other students were home for the holidays. Yet the Basilica of St. Francis Xavier in St. Louis was splendidly adorned for the holy season. Joyce's beauty radiated in a perfectly fitting Saks Fifth Avenue bride's dress borrowed from a friend, Ursula Decker, who had married my buddy Gene the previous June in New York. The basilica choir was present, and lo, the Rector of the medical school, Father Foote himself, said our wedding Mass and witnessed our wedding vows. Father Foote gave periodic short but lovely commentaries all through the ceremony; about the Church, about the season, about our marriage; our own Creation Day.

We had our wedding breakfast in classmate John Bouhassin's beautiful home with his entire extended family celebrating with us. They had adopted us for the moment. We have lost touch with the Bouhassins over the years, but our love and gratitude have not dimmed. John eventually became president of Cardinal Glennon Pediatric Hospital, a major part of Saint Louis University Medical School.

We even had a gala reception at my fraternity house hosted by our cook, Mrs. Maderaki, and attended by all of my in-town classmates, all fourteen of them.

Our 6-day honeymoon was in the nearby Pierre Marquette State Park, reached in classmate Bugsy Bugansky's '39 Chevy. It died when we got to the park and didn't wake up until we were ready to return.

Your great-aunt, Mary Joyce, arrived on October 26th early in my junior year and your uncle John, now with God, was born on June 8th the day after my graduation. Through it all, Joyce taught English in the St. Louis Public School System, masking as far as possible an almost constant state of pregnancy. That is how she supported our precarious budget of $14.50 per week for groceries and $35 monthly for rent. My mom and dad backed us up, so we really didn't feel the pinch. They kept us supplied with a blank check for emergencies. We were too busy for emergencies. Can I be blamed if I have always had a place in my heart for this lovely little poem by G. K. Chesterton?

Creation Day

Between our perfect marriage day
  And that fierce future, proud and furled
I only stole six days—six days:
  Enough for God to make the world.
For us is a creation made:
  New moon by night, new sun by day.
That ancient elm that holds the heavens
  Sprang to its stature yesterday.
Dearest and first of all things free,
  Alone as bride and queen and friend,
Brute facts may come and bitter truths;
  But here all doubts shall have an end.
Never again with cloudy talk
  Shall life be tricked or faith undone.
The world is many and is mad
  But we are sane and we are one.

It is because life is now being tricked that I write. Faith is now being undone. You are not permitted, my little lovely, to criticize too adversely the timing of our own Creation

Day. Had it not occurred precisely thus, you (et cetera implied) would not be receiving this letter.

If Mr. Chesterton could consider the world of his day mad, what might he think of our early 21st century world?

I have seen several motivating influences impacting our culture in my lifetime. Three, mentioned above, I consider the most prominent rudders steering our society into moral chaos. All have led to the attempted destruction of the American family. All have thus far been too successful.

The first factor was divorce and remarriage, establishing what became, in fact, serial polygamy. Social pressures abounded and at the Lambeth Conference of 1930 the Church of England removed restrictions on divorce. It was popularized by the media, Hollywood, the Press, etc. and led to the legalization of no-fault divorce. More than half of all marriages now are so doomed. The second rudder that, guiding our culture, profoundly assaulted the family, is contraception (also accepted at Lambeth). Contraception in one form or another has been with us throughout recorded history. The Church has always condemned it and it was denounced in the Old Testament of our Bible. However, intense, expensive, yet ultimately very profitable medical research discovered a way to poison a woman's reproductive system, rigging her up, as it were, for "safe" sex. This enhanced marital infidelity by giving further impetus to the pressure for divorce. There has been, by the way, no parallel attempt of chemical manipulation for men.

These two steering mechanisms led inevitably to the crowning cultural curse; abortion on demand. Although I will continue to use the term abortion, understand it as a euphemism. No one can deny that the preborn is living and thus has a soul, the principal source of the life, the livingness, imparted to otherwise inert chemicals. This is a member of a rational species, the human species, and is therefore a person, just like the rest of us. Having violated no law, moral, civil or otherwise, it is innocence personified, actually personified. To deliberately take the life of an innocent human person is murder. Although I will continue to use the term abortion for literary purposes, it cannot be legitimately denied: abortion is murder.

On May 12th, 1974, Mother's Day of that year, there was published in the *Washington Post* a message to the Supreme Court. Three hundred eighty two (382) physicians endorsed that message. It follows:

An Open Letter to the Supreme Court

Last Mother's Day, we published the first PHYSICIAN'S STATEMENT reasserting our commitment as physicians to the sanctity and dignity of human life. We have lived with your tragic decision contrary to that position for more than one year. We have lived; millions have died. We take this means of publicly communicating to you these basic facts which are fundamental to any informed decision regarding the unborn human person.

At the moment of fertilization there is formed in that one cell, a new human life. This new life is without question separate and distinct from either parent from whom it springs and is anew human being complete with respect to its entire physical potential. That this new being is both alive and human is neither a matter for debate nor for philosophical speculation. It is a biological fact not denied in any quarter of the informed scientific community.

The development of a human from fertilization to adulthood is a biologically smooth and continuous process. Cell by cell, minute-by-minute growth proceeds in an unrelenting and highly organized fashion. There is no specific point between fertilization and maturity where it can be said that "this particular cell" or "that particular minute" brought with it a humanity not previously present. Nothing but nourishment will be added from the world outside of the new being. All of the growth comes from within and all of it programmed into the master plan contained within that single fertilized cell.

Given this fact of life, we believe that it is not within the jurisdiction of any judge, however eminent his station, nor any theologian, however lofty his title, nor of any philosopher, however erudite his scholarship, to deny that the product of conception is both human and living. Nor is it within the purview of any physician, given that same fact of life, to establish himself as the arbiter of which life is to be considered "useful" or "meaningful."

We recognize that grave problems beset our society. We believe, however, that society may not cope with poverty, ignorance and disease by eliminating the poor, the ignorant and the lame. As physicians, we are committed to placing the highest conceivable value on each life that comes before us for our care. Our proper role is to accept the challenge of disease and to do whatever we can to help each life to function with dignity.

The Supreme Court and its fatal decision on January 22, 1973, in effect excused us from our commitment to our Hippocratic Oath. We assert that that oath represents a covenant between us and our patient. We seek no escape from its binding power. If the Supreme Court justices decide to still the problems of some by stilling the lives of others, that then is their decision. It is not ours. And neither by advice nor consent will we have part in it.

The choice before society is clear. Either human life must be viewed as having absolute value in and of itself and its dignity be cherished even in the face of adversity, or the value of life is only a relative thing and its destruction made subject to the whim and caprice of expediency. We, the undersigned, hereby take our stand for the sanctity and dignity of life along with our brother physician, Albert Schweitzer. Hear his words, and ponder their meaning for our society and for each member of that society: IF A MAN LOSES REVERENCE FOR ANY PART OF LIFE, HE WILL LOSE HIS REVERENCE FOR ALL LIFE.

There followed the names of the 382 sponsoring physicians. The ensuing years have seen a grim realization of Dr. Schweitzer's prophetic words. Our way of life has changed in coarse and ugly ways. It appears that the pivotal axis of this change has been not only the loss of reverence for human life, but also the resulting loss of reverence for the very bedrock of our society, the family itself. The birth rate has plummeted as the divorce rate has soared. Adolescence is prolonged and the time to be wedded postponed beyond the most fertile years and that critical time in which personal and social adjustments to the married life can be most easily made. Almost one third of all babies who are actually brought into birth in this country are born to single mothers and not into a family at all: no husband, no Daddy: what a burden. The number of couples living together without bothering to form a family by marrying actually challenges the number of those who marry. President Obama nullified the Defense of Marriage Act by publicly announcing that it will not be enforced. This was callous: overriding a law enacted by Congress and signed into law by a previous president. Some state courts—yes, courts—have enacted laws recognizing same-sex unions and calling them marriage. This was done against the express will of the states' citizens, ratified by legal ballot. Pornography addicts number in the tens of millions, again thanks largely to the Supreme Court. Child pornography has come of age and is now uncontrollable. Sodomy is no longer considered an illness, a sin or even unnatural, and pedophilia is trudging the same murky pathway to casual common acceptance.

Laws, taxes and society at large encourage mother to work away from her family, with daycare centers and ever earlier preschools managing a high percentage of young children during their most formative waking hours. It is not uncommon for a parent to drop off a sick child at the daycare center.

Daycare workers are hearing the baby's first words and witnessing his or her first step. These are (or ought to be) treasured family milestones. Then the parent, wearied and used from the day's work and bucking rush hour traffic to and from that work, arrives to reestablish her or his duty as mother and father. Is it right? Is it just?

Schools are educating in areas once strictly forbidden to any but the child's mother and father. In many school districts explicit sex education is taught in every grade, even the earliest: Sally has two mommies. In at least one state, California, sex education has been decreed a right of the school system not to be countermanded by the family. Your son or daughter must attend a grim portrait of things to come. That state also has enacted a law making it legal for a 12year-old to have herself vaccinated against a venereal disease without her parent's knowledge or permission. There have been deaths from that vaccine.

The American Academy of Pediatrics has actually recommended the distribution of poisonous birth control pills to 12 year old girls, darkly concealing it from the mother and the father. In New York City schools this is already being done. Where have all the doctors gone?

Draconian laws and their unelected judicial advocates have trampled our freedom of religion by "interpreting" it out of our constitution. This was our most basic and compelling founding freedom. Our Christian country is now by law anti-Christian.

Contraception has had a singular devastating effect on family life. The very phrase 'safe-sex' expresses a hidden condemnation of the dignity of the human person as well as the self-giving love expressed only in the beauty of marital sexual intercourse. Coupled with no-fault divorce, contraception completed the overture to the sexual revolution and rendered abortion inevitable.

Since the advent of the pill in the early 1960s, adultery, divorce, teenage sex, teenage pregnancy, venereal disease, pornography and deviant sexual practices including pedophilia have increased in tsunami fashion. Use of the pill is as common as salt. Knowledge of its poisonous effects is as uncommon as caviar. Among those poorly acknowledged effects is the ruin wrought on our understanding of the great dignity of being a human person.

Stalin once remarked that if you kill one person it is murder, but if you kill a million that is simply a statistic. Thus, we do not blanch when we recall that the Supreme Court has aided and abetted in the killing by physicians (physicians of a sort) of over 50 million human persons by way of surgical abortion. But the tragedy does not stop there.

At first, the pill was high in estrogen and therefore caused numerous heart attacks and strokes in women not previously susceptible to such maladies. This was costing the drug companies too much money in litigation. One company is known to have spent 65 million dollars in one year settling damage suits out of court; they don't want you to know. So the drug industry worked to bring the estrogen level down somewhat, but only somewhat, altering the drug's side-effect profile.

The pill now commonly in use does not necessarily stop contraception, but it does prevent the uterus from accepting the ovum by physiologically mimicking a state of pregnancy. By spoiling a woman's endocrine system, her body behaves as if it is already pregnant. The new human, when he or she arrives from the fallopian tube, having been a living human person for a week, is flushed out with the next menstrual cycle. No admittance and by its own mother.

Other side effects of the pill such as stroke, heart attacks, cancer, depression, weight gain, acne and so much more continue to fill page after page of the *Physician's Desk Reference*.

The dangerous problems are largely ignored and her physician neither properly nor honestly informs the woman.

Society imposes a disproportionate burden on women in the interests of "safe" sex. One may wonder for whom the safety is demanded. Is it the woman or the man who benefits more by this sham safety? It is not unusual for the man to pay for the abortion and then disappear in haste across the parking lot, abandoning the mother and their child to grim fate and not infrequently death. Planned Parenthood's abortion mills are least known for their cleanliness or their safety.

Based on the age of fertility, a reasonable number of couplings and the pharmacology of the pill, it is estimated that there are between 6 and 13 times as many contraceptive abortions as there are surgical ones. Do the math and gasp.

At a minimum, we have already aborted in one way or another a number of persons equal to the present population of the United

States. Thus following Stalin's logic, one stalwart of the Supreme Court could state, "You can't tell me that the single cell ovum is a person." That was just one more of his supreme decisions: he simply can't be told. He doesn't want to know. The right to life has been interpreted out of our Constitution. Can you doubt that liberty and the pursuit of happiness tremble nervously in the wings? We face a terror within: within our country, within our culture, within our hearts. We hardly know where to turn our sanctimonious faces from one outrageous nine-day wonder to the next. Yet none of this is happening in a vacuum.

The story of the horror of a ten-year-old boy in a prestigious university being sodomy raped by a school official who callously and repeatedly betrayed his trust sells some newspapers. It locks people to their TVs for a while, and then fades away from all except the ruined lives it leaves in its wake.

Twenty children murdered by a demented killer translates into changing gun laws and assaulting the long targeted Second Amendment. Never let a crisis go to waste. Political correctness protects things like sodomy and what the hate crime pundits prefer to call it when it victimizes the innocent young—intergenerational sex. That is all it takes anymore: just waiting—and doing nothing.

The descent of America into a secular abyss has proceeded at an accelerating pace for many decades and we, fools that we are, continue to look the other way. Militant atheism has been with us throughout recorded history, with its militancy accelerating continuously since the eighteenth century when science was said to have "liberated" itself and us from moral and religious constraints. This was a misrepresentation of true science but useful in the manipulation of culture. Consider a partial list of the scars it has left on the face of our society and its ultimate impact on family:

Fear of population (fear of people)

Theory of evolution replacing divine creation

Eugenics (a war on the weak and unwanted)

Radical feminism and its equally radical societal distortions, and thus, women's lib seeking to alter the normal role of the man and woman

No-fault divorce weakening marital commitment

Contraception

Abortion, the unjust, painful killing of a pre-born human person

The painful killing of a baby already born or in the process of being born

Premarital sex corrupting body and soul and of course the family

Politically correct language, sometimes mandated by law, corrupting truth

Use of euphemisms for the word sodomy to mask its evils

Removal of homosexuality from the DSM diagnostic standards manual of the American Medical Association causing untold harm

The birth of the acquired immune deficiency syndrome and its havoc

Judicial approval of pornography

Gigantic increase in STDs (the CDC statistics show that there are over 100 million permanent cases with 20 million new cases added yearly)

Judicial restriction of prayer and other religious practices

Usurpation of parental guidance and control of education

Explosion of sex and mind-corrupting violence in all popular entertainment outlets including movies, TV, computer games and handheld devices

- Sex education in all grades injuring the consciences of our children
- Cohabitation, one of the many onerous results of sex education in all grades
- Babies being born to unmarried women
- Legalization of sodomy mating in pretended marriages
- Euthanasia
- Isolation of the sick and the elderly
- Concentration of political power in a centralized government, weakening or even eliminating the principle of subsidiarity
- Increased use of alcohol and mind-altering drugs
- Callous abolition of the freedom of religion.

The list, of course, could go on. The point is that the family is the target.

All this, my sweet little Delaney, is a top-heavy preamble to pivotal questions asked all too infrequently:

1) What is a person? and

2) What is life?

Although brief, they are profound. Evading the answers has led to the plague partially outlined above.

Each human life has a distinct, personal and splendiferous point of origin. There is absolute continuity of that life in all of its phases of growth.

The life that is in you does not change from cell to cell, from organ to organ or from year to year. This was pointed out to the court in the doctor's letter a generation ago.

Your life is a divine gift replete with rights and obligations. There then remains the question of the source of the principle of life and obligations we and others may or must have to that Source. Our well cannot run dry. But enough for this first letter, my fairest one; know that I love you. I always will.

Letter No. 2

Answers to the Basic Questions of Life

My fairest child,

In my first letter, dearest one, I posed the problem of a world seemingly gone mad because its spiritual well has run dry. By the time you read these letters, the spiritual environment will have evolved, as cultures never remain stagnant. God alone knows, as I write this, what life will be for you and for families in your day. I repeat the truth with which I closed the first letter: our well cannot run dry. The flow underground is immense. God will never abandon us. In times of drought we must dig deeper. It is the will and not the well that actually dries.

In this letter, I attempt to answer the basic questions of life with which I closed your first letter. What is a person? – and What is life? They must be answered together. If you are a human being, you are ipso facto a human person. Those who have a need to justify abortion, contraception, human experimentation and the like, deny this of course.

The question of the intrinsic dignity of our neighbor does not arise until someone, such as an abortionist, has a reason to ignore or deny that dignity. It is immoral to take the life of an innocent person simply because you have decided that his death satisfies your ends.

It is similarly immoral in times of doubt to err on the side of possible evil. A hunter on seeing movement in a bush may not shoot at that bush simply because he guesses that the movement is caused by a deer. There may be a fellow hunter in there.

In his manner of justifying abortion, Justice Blackmun admitted that he was making such a guess. He was in doubt as to the beginnings of life and said so. He spoke of vague "penumbras" and "emanations," disingenuously guessing that the newly formed human was not a human at all. He and his colleagues pretended that they saw movement in the bush, and so the Supreme Court fired the shot that ended the lives of millions. Truly, truly, none are so blind as those who will not see.

Even in times of war, we have respected conscientious objectors and assigned noncombat duties to them. Men in battle also have had their qualms of conscience because of this inherent respect for human life.

May I tell you a little story about a man I knew well whose actions in World War II demonstrated to me that it is written in our hearts to know that life is a foundational treasure?

One freezing morning, he volunteered to repair broken phone lines to our troops in Bastogne during the Battle of the Bulge. He was thus isolated between the combatants as the battle raged around him. He reached the other troops and then volunteered again to go back, making certain that his work was secured.

At one point, he had to pass through a deep gulch in the terrain. Entering it, he suddenly discovered that he had become isolated with a weeping German soldier whose rifle rested several yards away. Both men were startled and fearful, but neither moved. Both pairs of eyes locked and after an interminable time, Bob, for that was his name, very slowly reached with two fingers to his breast pocket. Never taking his eyes off the obviously distraught German soldier, Bob drew a tiny pack of Lucky Strikes (only five GI issue) from the pocket and slowly offered one to the German. The enemy soldier was amazed and cautiously took the cigarette. They relaxed and smoked. Despite the pounding, the battle seemed rather distant. Bob handed the rest of the pack to that man. He then gave him the other little pack in his pocket, turned and climbed out of the gulch.

After the war, Bob was flown to Berlin for a special ceremony at which he was given medals by the USA, France and England for his bravery that morning. He was a true hero, but he couldn't kill a defenseless enemy soldier. I asked Bob whether he had been fearful that the German would shoot him as he left the gulch. Bob smiled and said rather whimsically, "You know, that thought never even crossed my mind."

There is within us a law inscribed in our natures at the core of our being. All peoples of all generations and places recognize it. That natural law is codified in the Ten Commandments. "Thou shalt not kill" is just one of its doctrines and is written upon our souls by our creator. God himself etched it in stone for Moses in the desert and for us in the Bible to guide us in our daily doings. There can be no peace, there can be no order, absent natural law. We should want to know then what it is about human life that renders us so sacrosanct among all the other living beings of our world. What is it that sets our species apart from and above all other species on earth? The answer lies in characteristics manifested only in the human species. Mankind can know, can doubt, can suspect, can question and reflect. In short, man can reason. We have operations that are manifestly spiritual, clearly revealing a spiritual soul, the principle from which these acts flow. We alone have the power to perceive and express rights and obligations.

It is not the prerogative of any particularly educated group of people, be they philosophers, scientists, physicians, lawyers or government officials, to decide for the rest of us who or what may be considered a human person. Each of the dissenters has an axe to grind, and the axe is at times bloody.

Your neighbor can be and usually is aware of a personal self. Deny it with dread. Embrace it with hope and courage. Life is a gift, a gift to which your right is absolute and may not be infringed upon. Though you be too young to know, though you be too sick to think, your right to life is absolute.

At what point in time did your personal life begin? The question is so obvious that it may appear strange or absurd. When did you become you?

In memory, we can see ourselves at ever earlier phases of our lives. Turn your mind back and look back through the years for the moment at which you became a human person. Look back and see the various milestones along which the person that you are has traveled. We see and can identify ourselves through adolescence, childhood, and infancy.

Surely none of these periods of Life conferred on you the quality of humanity that you did not already have. The magic moment could not have been birth itself, the first breath of life. Your human life had to have been intact else you could not have taken your first breath. You were undoubtedly the operative agent. The nine quiet months in your mother's womb witnessed the development of all of your vital interdependent organ systems; all of them living and all of them yours. If you are one of a set of twins or triplets who came naturally from the same conception, it can be assumed that that plan was written into the manuscript of life at the time of fertilization, a beautiful genetic trait that some few families possess.

It may not be claimed that your humanity commenced at the point at which the clump of cells called the blastomere emerged from the fallopian tube and implanted into the wall of your mother's uterus, for it was the same clump of cells it had been before it left the fallopian tube. It simply acquired a different source of nourishment and oxygen. It had within itself you had within yourself capacity to do this. Finally, with our retro spectroscope follow the mass of cells, ever diminishing in number, backward up the fallopian tube. No new cell carried within it some novel trait of humanity not previously present.

Look back until we see that first amazing cell, that spark of Life, the magic moment when your very personal and very human life began. Though you now be a hundred or more, all of you was there, hidden in that first splendid moment when you were conceived. That is our bird's-eye view of the continuum of life. Without doubt, a continuum it is. You are now; you were then and you will ever be, a human person.

More than a few scientists and theologians have ventured to redefine the beginning of Life. Some have chosen major stages of development such as implantation, the beginning of the nervous or the cardiovascular system or some other important step of embryonic development. There are those who assert that personal life can exist only after that vague and indefinite point when twinning is no longer possible. Many claim, improperly as we have seen, that life begins only at birth or when we take our first breath. These have condemned many little babies to a gruesome agony of death.

Others, such as James Watson, who with Francis Crick is given credit for the discovery of DNA, or Peter singer of Princeton University, have a different approach. They actually have written that they, or others of their stature and renown should be the ones qualified to determine whether this or that individual might qualify for personhood and the rights we have heretofore considered God-given. They have in mind that some children up to several years of age should be subject to their judgment on who is and who is not a human person and permitted, in their judgment, to live. They vigorously defend infanticide. Eugenics is not new. The curse of the war on the infirm and the poor has been with us throughout the centuries.

We must examine the instant of conception, for it is at this point that the journey of life begins for each of us. If we were to follow the new human through various significant changes in structure and function, we would note that at each change, the characteristic of singular, identifiable personal life remains unchanged. We will find that there is no moment; there is no special cell that carries with it some distinct marker of humanity not already present in the immediately previous moment or cell. It is important for you to bear in mind three characteristics of the two-cell stage of human development that are commonly overlooked. The very first cellular division expresses characteristics of the continuum of life that persist throughout all of life.

The first characteristic is that, oddly, there is no cell in human development that can truly be called the second cell. This may seem strange, but it is an important fact and it is true. When the first cell divides, it does not produce a second cell. Two cells of equal origin and importance simply emerge from that division. One did not come from the other. The first cell divided and became two, with the life of the first now abiding coextensive in both new cells. I will be describing the process called mitosis to you later, and you will see that the two daughter cells share equally in and are enlivened by the same property of life, the soul, that existed in the first or mother cell. The life itself always remains the same.

Bacteria and other primitive living things that have only one cell in their makeup are different. In their world, the first cell produces another separate cell, which it develops to be exactly like the first while remaining a distinctly other entity with its own particular life. Now we have a first and a second cell, exactly alike. They in turn are like two first cells and produce two more. Thus they soon become billions, and all images of the first.

Next you should know that the two second cells are united as one body. They cling to each other exactly as the cells of an adult person cling. Your body produces submicroscopic living protein structures called laminins. Laminins are essential to life. They are produced by the cell walls of every organ and tissue of your body. One of their several functions is to hold your tissues and organs together. Their form is exactly that of a cross, thus they have little arms with which they reach out across the intercellular space to grip and hold the adjacent sister cell.

Should the laminins of your body suddenly lose their grip, your body would become a shapeless glob on the floor. They hold all your cells, tissues and organs together, make them kind of sticky like Velcro. Therefore, your body when it had only two cells was a unit, and you may in truth refer to it as a body. (Aside: If you have access to a computer, Google "laminin" and be amazed.)

The third point is that at the two-cell stage some form of differentiation has already occurred. Only one of the two daughter cells has been programmed to form the cell, which will make you a three-cell person, at that time in your mother's body. The blueprint of your life was immediately working as planned. The fourth cell comes along a few hours later, but (with great importance) there is always a three-cell stage. Thus we know that when you were only two cells old:

1) Your life-giving principle was, and will remain, continuous.

2) Your body was a single unit.

3) The program of your life was already operative.

This was not so with those one-cell critters. So let us get on to the fascinating biology.

Biology

We cannot study life without being introduced to that biological wonder of life, the chromosome. What a chromosome is and what it does ought to move us to wonder, for it is a marvel of great importance, beauty and complexity.

Each of the millions of cells in our body has in its nucleus 23 pair of these marvels.

Our distinguishing chromosomal number is 46. That identifies the human species. The chimpanzee has 48 chromosomes. Thus, even microscopically, we can already readily distinguish the species.

The chromosomes in bone tissue are exactly the same as the chromosomes in brain tissue. The cells in the various organ systems of the adult are specialized in obeying the master plan written into the conceptus, the first cell, and thus differentiate in development into the myriad tissues and organs. The blueprint, however, the information inscribed into the original cell, remains absolutely unchanged in all subsequent cells.

And looking through his electron microscope, the biologist sees the chromosomes as 23 pairs. These are strands of proteins twisted together like a barber pole. One strand—let's say the white one—comes from the mother and the red from the father. These strands carry the genetic information that gives you your identity. Whether you are male or fe-

male, tall or short, black or white or whatever, all your identifying biology is present,
encoded, in those marvelous little twisted
strands. It makes no difference whether it is a
heart cell, a skin or liver cell. It is worth repeating: all of your chromosomes are exactly
the same and are in no way different from
that very first cell with one of the strands derived from your mother's ovum and the other
from your father's sperm. The father's sperm
carries the marker that will determine the sex
of the baby.

When they meet, however, ovum and
sperm do not have complete double-stranded
chromosomes. In their formation, the mother
and father's chromosomes unwind and the
resulting chromosomes remain distinct. On
further division, the new cells have only sin-
gle-stranded chromosomes, 23 of course, as
they were when each was one half of a pair.
Thus the ovum and sperm wind up with 23
chromosomes.

There is an Olympian race to form that master cell initiating each of Our Lives. Millions and millions of sperm cells rushing and swirling their whip-like tails, swimming frantically to reach queen egg.

She lives within her cell wall, a tent-like shell, her "zona pellucida"—zone of peace and light, as it is called. After she is expelled from the ovary, she floats into the fallopian tube, which has finger-like structures to gather her up as a child's hand might gather up a little piece of candy or a newly hatched chick.

The instant that the champion sperm reaches her zona pellucida and starts to penetrate it, that shelter changes, hardening in a way that forbids entry to all competitors of her champion. He locks the door behind him. He is hers and she is his. Thus occurs fertilization, the emergence of new life.

Seems simple, doesn't it? A new and unique cell is formed. A new and unique human comes into being. The chromosomes from mother and father meet and embrace, forming spectacularly personal new chromosomal marriages. The factory whistle blows and the waltz begins; work begins. Life, your life, begins.

It is worth repeating. When that one sperm enters the ovum, all other suitors are excluded as the cell wall, the pellucida, of the ovum suddenly becomes hard and forbids entry to all other sperm cells.

There is now a new member of the human species, distinct from any previous human since Adam, whose like will never reappear to the end of time. As another old song truthfully proclaims, "There'll never be another you."

The new cell is busy with the microscopic doings of its life. There are tiny factories, the mitochondria, making precisely the proper complex proteins and materials to build the next cell. There are messengers traveling back and forth, into and out of headquarters, the nucleus. The messengers carry blueprints, materials and templates to the factories. There are biological gatekeepers at the cell wall and the nuclear wall permitting only the proper material and porters in and out. There is so much more. It is truly amazing. I envy the biologist studying this wondrous complexity. And wonder of Wonders: It lives. It takes on and metabolizes nourishment for it-self and its progeny. It grows. It reproduces. It is alive and has a goal.

First we will look into just why we can state that it is living. Then we can examine its claim to be a person. The picturing of the first cell division is paramount as it prefigures all of the cell divisions that will follow. It clearly attests to the continuity of life and the sameness of that life in all future cells.

As you have seen, it immediately prefigures specialization of cells, which will become tissues and organs, as the first two daughter cells are not quite exactly alike. Remember, one of them is specialized to divide first and the other to divide later. There is that three-cell stage.

Matter is matter, merely that and nothing more. Of itself, it is not living. Matter does not grow, nor does it feed. It does not metabolize food or reproduce. Sodium will remain sodium, and chlorine will remain itself. Mix them under certain conditions, and they may become salt for your table, but manipulate them as you may, they will not come to life.

Working with chemicals to produce living matter has been tried and tried expensively and extensively. Thus far, we have failed. Pinocchio will always be only a charming wooden boy in a fairy tale and never could be a real boy. Its worth stressing: matter of itself is lifeless.

Yet your first cell, the conceptus, you of just so many years ago, that tiny cell, had its own life, your own life. It metabolizes food, utilizing oxygen from its environment. Through division after division after division of its cells in strict obedience to the blueprint encoded in the first cell, the new human being matures. The cells eventually specialize into brain, heart, bone, skin or whatever. It has a plan. As we observed, specialization is not new to the developing human. Yet through each splitting of the cells, the life, the livingness and personal singularity of the matter will remain itself; unchanged as clearly attested to by its DNA, its chromosomes.

Your atmosphere today is the air around you, but the atmosphere of the conceptus is the constantly warm pellucida as it is being ushered through the fallopian tube. Its nutrients are supplied from the contents of the ovum. (How like a mother, to bring along enough food for the trip.) The pellucida itself does not expand, and thus the cells become proportionately smaller during the short week they remain in their shelter. Thus energy is conserved and access through the tube is maintained. So, like a grain field in the wind, the little hair-like cilia, the wallpaper of the fallopian tube, are waving, singing, urging and cheering the new human, ushering him or her on to a temporary home in the wall of the womb. The doctor will call that wall the endometrium of the uterus.

We must now view this first cell splitting and observe that the life of the soul, which informs and thus animates the otherwise inert matter, does not and in fact cannot change. Picture the cell as a ball and the nucleus as a little ball within a bit like the yolk of an egg. The nucleus is the office or headquarters. The cell is breathing. As said, it takes in oxygen and discharges carbon dioxide, thus interacting with its "atmosphere" just as you do.

The cell is a beehive of activity. Its little factories, the messengers, engineers and guards work away at their assigned duties. After a time, all appears to become disarranged and the contents seem to mill about in confusion. They are, in fact, working from a plan. That is, they are biologically directed. The wall of the nucleus disintegrates and its contents spill out to mingle with their cell mates. The barber pole unwinds. The mother's white band assembles a new red made from the material either already there while in the tube or later brought into the cell by the guarded portals in the cell wall and manufactured to the specifications of headquarters. The red band follows suit. Each band assembles a new partner from the material of the cell and clings to this new mate with a little belt-like attachment. This is the waltz of life. The new partners drift to opposite sides of the cell and the cell itself begins to cave in between them.

While all this is going on in the cell's stew of Life, the animating principle, the soul, is and must be constant throughout as it is operative throughout the entire realigning cell now forming into two new cells. The continuity of Life, the "sameness" of the life in both sides of the cell, is of paramount importance. It is important because it declares the "continuum of life" which remains constant throughout all the billions of future cell divisions in a lifetime. The soul never changes.

The caving-in process proceeds as if some belt were squeezing into the center portion of the cell with the two reforming barber poles on either side. It is an imaginary belt, of course. The caving-in is the result of the cell contents relining and drifting apart to opposite sides of the cell. This entire process of cell division is called mitosis. It is the name given to all regular cell divisions throughout a lifetime.

Becoming ever tighter, the belt ultimately separates the two halves. But they are not in reality halves. They are now complete separate cells. Understanding this point is crucial. The life principle animating that very first cell never diminished or changed. It is precisely the same life-source now enlivening two daughter cells. Thus there are two cells where there had been but one. It cannot be said of either of the two new cells that one is mother and the other daughter for neither derived from the other. It may only be said that where there had been but one, there are now two cells. The lamins of the new cells reach out their little arms to hold the sister cells tight. They form one body. They are sheltered in the same tent, which guarded the mother's ovum and then refused admission to all sperm cells other than the father's sperm. The zone of peace, her tent, will remain sheltering the new life through all of its cell divisions on its way to its new home in the womb. As said, the size of this little pellucida, the tent, remains the same.

While they are in the fallopian tube, the cells become proportionately smaller with the same life sustaining all. The principle of life, the soul, has not changed. It animates completely each cell and all future cells. Repetitive perhaps, but it is important to stress that the life force, the soul, is contiguous and continuous.

And so: What is a person? and What is life? Perhaps it is more to the point to ask: Who is a person? If you have followed, you will understand that human life defines personhood.

The answer then is not difficult. You are! You are a person. You are a person and so your life is inviolable. It has been from the time of that magic meeting in your mother's fallopian tube. This is a gift from an almighty and all-loving Creator. No one is privileged to remove it from you. Let me repeat from that letter of the physicians to the Supreme Court one year after they fired their lethal shot.

The development of a human from fertilization to adulthood is a biologically smooth and continuous process. Cell by cell, minute-by-minute growth proceeds in an unrelenting and highly organized fashion. There is no specific point between fertilization and maturity where it can be said that "this particular cell" or "that particular minute" brought with it a humanity not previously present. Nothing but nourishment will be added from the world outside of the new being. All of the growth comes from within and all of it programmed into the master plan contained within that single fertilized cell.

Given this fact of life, we believe that it is not within the jurisdiction of any judge, however eminent his station, nor any theologian, however lofty his title, nor of any philosopher, however erudite his scholarship, to deny that the product of conception is both human and living. Nor is it within the purview of any physician, given that same fact of life, to establish himself as the arbiter of which life is to be considered "useful" or "meaningful."

And so my fairest, it was important to the harbingers of death—death to the person; death to the family—to confuse the issue of the origin and the meaning of life. It was important for abortionists of any stripe to mask their menace and to euphemize the murder of the innocent by calling it abortion or termination of pregnancy.

Thus our next question—How did we get here?—and its logical corollary—Why are we here anyway?—swell to overpowering importance. They are overpowering because unless they are honestly and openly addressed, life becomes, as the Supreme Court would have it, a penumbra or something equally vague. The way of the family then recedes. A veritable descent into a maelstrom. This grim destiny is neither for you nor for me. It need not and should not be for any human person.

It will be the subject of your next letter. Until then, know that I love you. Wherever I am, I am praying for you.

GGDD

XXX

Letter No. 3

An Overview of How and Why the Family Has Been the Target of Evil Influence

My fairest child,

The question of the day: Why are we here? What is our purpose and our path?

Life is a song that never ends and each must sing his own. Rhetoric? Perhaps, but music and poetry are part of my letter to you and I pray they will be with you always. And yet I have no song to give you, my little one. For it is true; each must sing his own. It could be, in fact, more a dirge than a song. Whether it will be either a song or a lament will, in the end, be your choice.

How did we—we—get to where we are? I speak, of course, not of the personal biology but rather the societal question. How did we, our society, get to the point of ignoring or even denying the existence of our Creator and actually resenting His "intrusion" into our daily affairs?

Only yesterday, I heard a profound and holy Bishop castigate our government for its role in the assault on the family. Despite the fact that it was a sermon during Holy Mass and applause is not the ordinary or expected response, the people in the pews rose to their feet and thunderously applauded their approval.

Yet they—we—are a sect apart. We live in a type of moral ghetto and do not speak for society at large. As I write this, the vast majority of Christians are Christians only nominally and do not look to the faith to direct their daily tasks. The travails of the family remain and, as our Bishop pointed out, are increasing.

And so, my little one, this letter is meant to give you an overview of how and why the beautiful institution known as family has been the target of evil influence. Your own potential influence on its rescue will not be part of this letter, but hopefully will follow.

Whether your response will be a lament or a song will indeed be your choice. A lament is a dirge of defeat, a willingness to lose hope. Your song, come what may, can be a song of holy war, war against evil, a battle cry wherein we rise to our feet with our Bishops; with the church. I say I have no song to give you because the song that we are to sing to an adverse, even a perverse world is not mine to give. It was given to us two thousand years ago by Jesus: "Have courage. I have over-come the world." Again, in the very first book of the Old Testament our Creator says to a 99-year-old Abraham, "I am God, the Almighty. Walk in my presence and be blameless." Our well of faith and hope cannot will not run dry. It is His well. It is His gift.

We have merely to want it and to ask Him for it.

Even as the bishop composed his homily, the assault of the family continued and now increases in force. Well aware of its tragic sequellae, the American Academy of Pediatrics has proclaimed its approval of sodomy, declaring their official decision that it is not abnormal. They have also sanctioned the unsupervised permission for little girls of any age to secretly purchase birth control pills known to be poisonous, carcinogenic and homicidal. Organized and official pediatrics says "Yes!"

Where have all the doctors gone? The Supreme Court, not adverse to thwarting the will of the people by "interpreting" the Constitution, has declared the Defense of Marriage Act to be unconstitutional. For them now, political correctness supplants the law and the Constitution. Thus they give their approval to sodomy and all of its ultimate and inevitably harmful consequences.

From the Book of Genesis: "Now the serpent was more subtle than any of the beasts on earth." And so it is, my little one. Ever since the day man first decided to be like God, there has always been a most subtle serpent redefining the meaning of "blameless" and urging us not to walk in the presence of God. The story of the serpent's efforts to obscure our moral heritage has been persistent and distinct. It is recorded in the Bible. We have seen it in the history of nations. We see it now quite clearly in the characteristics, distinguishing attitudes, habits and beliefs of our world.

The serpent was subtle enough to influence one-third of the angels of heaven to follow him into hell. He was subtle enough to influence our first parents to abandon their divine legacy, what was to have been our inheritance, and instead leave us with the heritage of sin and death.

Yet his subtlety will not and cannot prevail. It cannot conquer the Man on the Cross.

This letter will be a very brief overview of the serpent's subtle pathway in order to show you how we got this way. (Should documentation be helpful, I will include a reading list that may help to clarify points of particular interest.)

In his "Letters to Families," as in his Apostolic Exhortation *"Familliaris Consortio,"* St. John Paul II pointed out that God in His trinitarian nature exists as one God comprising a community of love in three divine persons: Father, Son and Holy Spirit. It should not be surprising, then, that in creating man in His own image, God sanctions and blesses that community of persons—the family. It will also surprise no one that the serpent in his subtle rage will target the family in his rebellion against his and our Creator.

As I promised, my dearest one, your letter is not meant to be a philosophical or scientific treatise.

The history of man's rebellion at the urging of the enemy commenced in the Garden and continues today.

I have no idea, little one, whether Sir Isaac Newton actually sat in the shade of an apple tree and questioned why the apple that fell on his head did not fall up instead of down. Sir Isaac, however, opened vast fields of scientific inquiry. He was originally regarded as a philosopher, and I doubt the term "scientist" was much in use in his day.

Although ancient astronomers had cast some suspicion that our planet earth was not the center of the universe, it remained for Copernicus and Galileo in the 16th century to give more tangible evidence for this fact of nature. It was actually not until the 19th century and the use of more advanced telescopes that this now well-known concept advanced from "hypothesis" through "theory" to be accepted and finally proven as scientific "law."

That growth of knowledge over the centuries was facilitated by the ever increasing availability of documentation, communication and automated printing. This, combined with the veritable explosion of scientific knowledge and technology, had the tendency to separate science from philosophy from the 17th to the 20th centuries.

Science tends to build upon science. One man's discovery leads to the solution to another man's inquiry. Thus we have progressed from prisms and magnifying glasses to the Hubble Space Telescope. We have learned that not even our sun is the center of the universe. The whole thing started from the explosion of a tiny micro-microscopic "something" thirteen-and-a-half billion years ago. "Scientific proof" became society's basis of truth, of what must be believed—how very subtle.

While science was thus advancing over the years, giving us ever more efficient means of communication and transportation, cities and nations became ever more concentrated centers of production and trade. Our factories, railroads, highways and ever so much more that we take for granted were not so long ago not even imaginable. It took Magellan's crew over three years to complete the first effort of man to go around the world. He himself did not survive the trip. Now astronauts fly around it willy-nilly while they are eating their lunch.

Until the next letter, my fairest one; know that I love you. I always will.

Letter No. 4

The Amazing Biology Showing We Are Wondrously Made:

The Gift of Life— A Life That Is Human

WE are wondrously, marvelously made. Should you be privileged to enter any of the tens and tens of trillions of those cells which are your body's building blocks and look about, as you might had you entered some surreal city or special museum, astonishment would be your immediate and continuous reaction. Factories, repair shops, delivery trucks are in abundance throughout the cell. It has traffic control, sewage disposal and an astounding computer system unmatched by any of our industrial giants.

There is more, so much more to anchor you in utter fascination. The city has a capitol, the nucleus. That nucleus is precisely the same in each of those 30 or so trillion cells throughout your body and remains so throughout your life. It is here that your digital operating system functions. As noted, your computer system is the envy of any and all of those computer giants. Not one of them, nor all of them combined, can begin to match your little cells' digital operating prowess. Information input, storage and retrieval barely hint at your cell's normal abilities. Proofreading, splicing, shredding, replication and repair technology as well as information compression are constants within us throughout our lives. Permit me a "wow." And remember that each nucleus is the identical twin to your very first cell's nucleus at the time of conception and to all of that cell's descendants.

Life goes on, and we remain comfortably unconscious of its complex proceedings. If our digital operating system should fail at any link in its vital chain, life could not exist. This is true not only of your life and mine it is also true of all cellular species of life.

All of the hundreds and thousands of proteins of which your body is composed and on which it depends are made up of four and only four acids called nucleic acids. Our digital technology is built into two molecular marriages, namely C to G and A to T. That is cytosine to guanine and adenine to thymine. These two couplings are the building blocks of the digital operating system for you and for any other living thing on this earth, be it a giant sequoia, a minuscule one-celled germ, an elephant or a blade of grass. Prominent universities have spent dozens of years and millions of dollars trying to show experimentally how those two marriages might have occurred spontaneously in nature some three-and-a-half billion years ago. They have failed and as far as I know have given up trying. It is worth repeating and, in fact, savoring we are indeed wonderfully, marvelously made.

We daily add to our body three things: water (we carry our ocean within us), food and air. These pass along those tiny marvelous cells contained in your various organs. The cells of those organs recognize, extract and process what is needed and either within the cell itself or by way of your bloodstream, send their finished products to the organs where they are functional.

Getting air seems simpler. Basically, we breathe in nitrogen and oxygen and breathe out carbon dioxide with the same nitrogen that carried the oxygen in. The nitrogen is just a minute carrier, but we couldn't live without it.

Precisely then, when does life actually start? How does it get its food, oxygen and water before it has the ability to breathe or eat? Is your life totally singular, unique? Or is it in some way a continuation of the life that existed in your mother or your father? These are fundamental questions.

We speak in our Constitution of the "right to life." This is not a right ascribed to all living things. No one would realistically suppose that harvesting a field of wheat or corn involves depriving the wheat or corn of an inviolable right. This is also true of the use of beef or pork products bringing meat to the table. None of these living animal creatures has a rational sense of awareness or self, nor have they a sense of rights and obligations. That sense can only be demonstrated in the human species. Eating a BLT is not a crime. Animals, of course, also need the protection of pain, which can serve as a means of recognition of danger. Our farmers and providers are careful to avoid causing pain.

Neither egg nor sperm are human beings. Both are products of human life derived from separate persons. Many vital products of your life, while essential to that life, are continually produced, used, disposed of and replaced.

The products of your salivary, lacrimal, pancreatic and sweat glands are a few of the enormous number of examples.

The egg and the sperm are members of this group. They differ in that while they are not vital to the life of the persons producing them, they are causal to a separate life as well as to the life of their particular species. It is, or rather will be, a life that is demonstrably and totally distinct from those two lives on which their production was dependent. And that brings us to a new and truly life-giving term —Syngamy. You won't need a medical dictionary for that one. It simply means a coming together of two gametes, one from the mother and one from the father.

The egg and the sperm do not contribute in any way to the vitality of the two people whose own lives are responsible for their production. The mother produces several hundred eggs by the time of her adolescence and disposes of one of them with her periods each month until her menopause. The man constantly produces sperm by the hundreds of millions and continually disposes of them either spontaneously or by stimulation. In neither case are they essential to the life that formed them.

Strange World: Never before have people appeared so very sure of themselves. Throughout this earth, we seem to have no objection to the slaughter of human life by numbers so great that they cannot be comprehended. Consider millions and billions of little ones not even permitted to leave the womb of their mother alive; this passes not as a denial of their right to life, the most basic of all natural rights, but merely the acceptance of another statistic. Was it not Stalin who said that if you kill one person it is murder, but if you kill a million it is only another statistic? He then proceeded to kill tens of millions. The denial of natural law will not proceed without grave consequences. The right to life is the most basic of those laws built into our nature and thus shared universally by all members of the human species. Without this, no other right has or can have meaning.

My dearest one, know that I love you. Wherever I am, I am praying for you.

GGDD

XXX

Tribute (*Catholic Standard*, November 29, 2018)

Dr. Richard Delaney remembered for his love for his patients, his faith

By Maureen Boyle, Special to the Standard

REFLECTING on the beautiful image of Our Lord, the great physician, who in His abundant compassion healed the sick in mind, body and soul, immediately draws to mind the late Dr. Richard P. Delaney who for nearly 60 years in the Montgomery County region of the Archdiocese of Washington, practiced family medicine with Jesus Christ the Divine healer as his perfect model and guiding light.

After a prolonged cancer illness, Dr. Delaney died at the age of 90 on the morning of October 28th at Holy Cross Hospital. His beloved family, multitudes of friends, as well as former colleagues and patients, were among the hundreds of mourners who attended a Mass of Christian Burial at St. Bernadette Parish, Silver Spring, on November 3rd.

"He was a man among the greatest I've ever known... the Light of Christ shown through every part of his life," said Father James Gould, pastor of St. John the Evangelist, Warrenton, Virginia, who served as the homilist during the funeral Mass.

Echoing the words of Matthew 25:36 when Jesus said, "For I was sick and you cared for me," the priest said, "All of you took the place of Jesus Christ in the life of this doctor…(He) gave so much to all of us."

A native of Wyoming, Pennsylvania, Dr. Delaney was one of six children. After graduating high school, he spent two years serving in the US Army and was stationed in South Korea. When he returned from military service, he graduated from the University of Scranton, where he majored in Biology. Following his 1957 graduation from St. Louis University Medical School, Dr. Delaney earned an internship at Providence Hospital in Washington, DC, after which he began his almost six decades long Family Medical Practice in the Silver Spring–Wheaton area.

It was during his service in South Korea, he received his vocation to practice medicine, said Joyce Delaney, his beloved wife of 64 years. While riding in the back of a military transport truck, he noticed a Korean woman, a leper, being chased and harassed by her fellow villagers. Dr. Delaney jumped out of the truck, scolded the woman's tormentors, comforted her and gave her the only valuable thing he had—a pack of cigarettes so she could sell them to get medical aid.

At that very moment, he realized he wanted to spend the rest of his life helping people, Joyce Delaney told the Catholic Standard, while sitting at the kitchen table of the Silver Spring home where she and Dr. Delaney lived for more than 50 years and where they raised their eight children.

For that life-changing event, the many hundreds of patients myself and several family members included whom Dr. Delaney went on to treat with the same care and compassion, consider themselves blessed beyond measure.

I will be forever grateful for Dr. Delaney's compassionate care especially when elderly family members were in their later years. In my father's final illness, Dr. Delaney reminded me to send for a Catholic priest, but at the same time he made darn sure the much-younger doctors treating my ninety-year-old dad knew we were not going to give up on life sustaining treatments. I'll never forget Dr. Delaney telling me, "You have to fight for your dad. No matter what, you fight for life."

Dr. Delaney also served as a founder and longtime physician for Holy Cross Hospital Hospice, which offers end-of-life care for patients in their homes, assisted living or nursing home facilities. At a time in his life and career when he had earned a well-deserved day off to rest and relax, Dr. Delaney spent every Thursday making house calls for patients near and far whom he treated with dignity and kindness as their earthly lives were nearing the final stages. At the end of life, some doctors dismissed their longtime patients, said Joyce Delaney, recalling why her husband served in hospice care right up until the end of his medical profession. He especially wanted to take care of people when they had no one care for them, she said.

During regular office visits, Dr. Delaney's always cheery, "How ya doing, Kid?" brightened your mood no matter what ailed you. In his office, sweet photos were displayed of the doctor's cherished family that grew to 34 grandchildren and 20 great-grandchildren. His Irish eyes would smile as he spoke so proudly and lovingly of all their comings and goings.

After an exam, there was often a prescription written, but even longer and more meaningful conversations about the Catholic faith, history and American politics would ensue. Dr. Delaney was a courageous and faithful defender of human life from conception to natural death, as well as the Church's teachings on marriage and the family.

A longtime parishioner of the Shrine of St. Jude Parish, Rockville, Dr. Delaney was also

a member of Opus Dei. For decades, he was a
6:30 a.m. daily mass goer at Saint Bernadette
Parish, where in recent years he also attended
Sunday Mass. My family and I had the privi-
lege of attending the same weekly Mass at St.
Bernadette's as the Delaneys.

No doubt Dr. Delaney for whom we will
continue to pray and whose life, faith and
profession were entirely united and guided
by his great love for Christ, the Good Doctor, the Blessed Mother and the Church will
still look after his patients, serving as an inter-
cessor from the Father's house. "This is what
he worked for his whole life," said Joyce Delaney.

Dr. Delaney was predeceased by his oldest
son John, who died in 2006, and his grand-
son Luke Loria, who passed away in 1997. In
addition to his wife, he is survived by seven
children, Mary Joyce Cable (Joe), Ann
Collins (F.J.), Eileen Loria (Dick), Maureen
Crumley (Mike), Patrick, Michael (Michelle)
and Richard (Kira), 34 grandchildren and 20

great-grandchildren. Interment was in Gate of Heaven Cemetery, Silver Spring.

About the Author

Richard Delaney was the beloved husband of Joyce Delaney and father of eight children. At the time of his death on October 28, 2018, he was the grandfather of thirty-four and the great-grandfather of twenty. For sixty years, Dick was a physician of renown as a general practitioner. He was founder of the Hospice in Holy Cross Hospital. His defense of the unborn—based on the evidence of medicine and science—was profound, irrefutable, and publicly shared by many physicians in the Washington area. Anyone who knew him was soon aware of his profoundly humble and holy heart. Before every patient's encounter, he would pray "Let me treat this person as if I were treating you, Lord Jesus." His patients knew him as their personal friend, some from birth through second generations. His care for the dying was his special concern and he often spent his chosen "day off" visiting the homes of those in hospice. Dick also drew his most experienced medical friends together to help deepen their spiritual lives. His peers considered him to be a "great doctor" and a "great man."

DOCTOR RICHARD DELANEY was a man of multiple loves: he loved his God, he loved his Church, he loved his wife and family, and he loved his patients and served them with a unique brand of holistic medicine that embraced both their spiritual and their physical well being. In a special way, too, he loved life. In this short, powerful book, cast in the form of letters to a beloved grandchild, he expounds on his deep and abiding love for this most fundamental of human goods from the special perspective of a skilled physician appalled by the casual disrespect for life now abroad in society.

——Russell Shaw, Author,
American Church and other books

Here DR. DICK DELANEY distills a testimony designed to penetrate the minds and hearts of his grandchildren and those they will beget. He pours the heart of a Christian Hippocrates, a scientist, and a philosopher into this work, to show them what it means to love the creation God has placed around us. His descendants are blessed to have this, and older readers will wish to emulate him, even if only half as well.

—Dr. Patrick Fagan, Director of
Marriage and Religion Research Institute,
Catholic University of America

RICHARD DELANEY lived a life rich with meaning, and in this little book he shows us all how to lead meaningful lives. Dr. Delaney saw God's love at work even on the cellular level. He saw, too, the consequences of our violations of love's order. His is wisdom worth passing on to the next generation."

——Mike Aquilina,
Author and Television Host

Made in the USA
Middletown, DE
02 May 2024